MW00824274

Published by Bassline Publishing
www.basslinepublishing.com

ISBN 13: 978-1-912126-43-9

Notation Legend

The Stave: most music written for the bass guitar uses the bass clef. The example to the right shows the placement of the notes on the stave.

Tablature: this is a graphical representation of the music. Each horizontal line corresponds with a string on the bass guitar, with the lowest line representing the lowest string. The numbers represent the frets to be played. Numbers stacked vertically indicate notes that are played together. Where basses with five or six strings are required, the tablature stave will have five or six lines as necessary.

Notes shown in brackets indicated that a note has been tied over from a previous bar.

Repeats: the double line and double dot bar lines indicate that the music between these bar lines should be repeated. If the music is to be repeated more than once, a written indication will be given i.e. 'play 3x'.

1st & 2nd Time Endings: these are used for sections that are repeated, but which have different endings. The first ending is used the first time, the second is used on the repeat. The first ending is ignored on the repeat, only the second is used.

Slap: the note is slapped with the thumb.

Pop: the note is popped with either the first or second finger.

Thumb Up: played with an upstroke of the thumb.

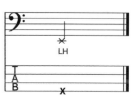

Fretting Hand: played by hammering on with the fretting hand.

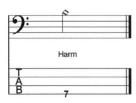

Harmonic: note is played as a harmonic by lighting touching the string above the fret indicated.

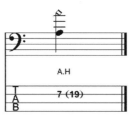

Artificial Harmonic: fret the lower note and tap the string over the fret shown in brackets.

Trill: alternate between the notes indicated by repeatedly hammering-on and pulling-off.

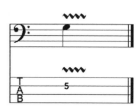

Vibrato: the pitch of the note is altered by repeatedly bending and releasing the string.

Hammer-On: only the first note is struck. The second is sounded by fretting it with another finger.

Pull-Off: Only the first note is struck. Lift the fretting finger to sound the second fretted note.

Slide: play the first note, then slide the finger to the second.

Picking Hand Tap: note is tapped with a finger of the picking hand. If necessary, the finger will be specified.

Fretting Hand Tap: note is tapped with a finger of the fretting hand. If necessary, the finger will be specified.

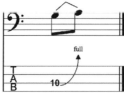

Bend: note is bent upwards to the interval indicated. ½ = half step, full = whole step.

Bend and Release: note is bent up to the interval indicated then released to the original note.

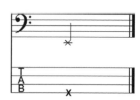

Ghost Note: note is a pitchless 'dead' note used as a rhythmic device.

Accent: note is accentuated, or played louder.

Staccato: note is played staccato - short.

Tenuto: note is held for its full length.

p   *piano* - played very softly
mp   *mezzo-piano* - played moderately quietly
mf   *mezzo forte* - played moderately loud/strong
f   *forte* - played loud/strong

D.C al Coda: Return to the beginning of the song and play until the bar marked Coda. Then jump to the section marked Coda.
D.S al Coda: Return to the sign, then play until the bar marked Coda. Then jump to the Coda.
D.C (or D.S) al Fine: Return to the point specified, then play until the Fine marking. Stop at this point.

Contents

Introduction

Welcome to *The Bass Guitarist's Guide to Reading Music: Beginner Level*, the first of three books that will teach you to read music on the bass guitar. Whether you are a newcomer to reading, or if you already have a little experience, you should find that this book is an invaluable resource for developing your reading skills.

The ability to read music is one of the most important skills to master for an aspiring professional musician. Learning to read fluently will open up many areas of employment that would previously have been unavailable to you – session work, theatre shows, touring and function band work are all examples of paid, professional engagements which require reading musicians. Being able to read also means that you will be able to fill in for other bass players on short notice, as well as write and arrange parts for your own bands – both invaluable skills. Music is a highly competitive industry and in order to succeed in it you should look to find every advantage that you can over your competition. Being the best reader that you can be is an excellent way to do this.

I have written this series of books because after teaching both privately and in music schools for several years I have noticed that there is a distinct lack of material available for bass guitarists who want to learn to read. Many of the books that are available contain predominantly dull, scale-based exercises, with almost no explanation as to *how* you should go about learning to read them. Similarly, very few contain explanations of musical features such as navigation, key signatures, time signatures or dynamics. In this book you'll find that all of these things are covered in detail and are supported by an extensive selection of exercises which will allow you to work on them in a musical way.

Audio Files

This book is also unique in that it includes audio files for all of the exercises, which are available to download free of charge from the Bassline Publishing website. Whilst I believe that it is important to work on sight reading exercises predominantly with just a metronome, many of my students have raised the valid point: 'how do I know if I'm playing it right?!' The audio files therefore exist as a valuable reference point for you to use to check the accuracy of what you are playing when studying without a teacher present.

To download the audio files, go to www.basslinepublishing.com and log in – if you don't have an account, you'll need to create one. Once logged in, click on FREE Stuff on the main menu. You'll find the audio in a zip file listed under the bonus content for this book.

The majority of the audio consists of bass guitar recorded with only a metronome rather than a full backing track. This has been done to encourage you to learn to keep your place within the score without the safety net of an obvious drum pattern to help you. However, the ten 'real world' exercises at the end of the book are recorded with a full band backing track so that you can put what you have learnt to the test in a more realistic environment. These tracks are available in two forms – with bass and without. You can use the bass tracks for reference if needed, and the backing tracks to play along with.

How to Use This Book

Before you can hope to read music, you must first learn to understand the language in which it is written. This book aims to teach the fundamentals of this language and illustrate them through examples and exercises.

The important thing for you – the reader – to be aware of is that you are not expected to 'sight-read' any of the exercises in this book. Sight reading comes with time and practice, once you have studied the language of music in detail. Instead, these exercises are to be **studied**: when you make a mistake, you should stop and consider what you did wrong: refer to the audio if you need to or discuss the problem with a teacher. Once you have corrected the mistake, move on. You should keep working through each piece in this manner, until you can play it by following the notation. In doing so you will be absorbing the language of written music and learning from the mistakes that you make. The ability to read a piece of music on sight will develop naturally as you follow this path of study.

You should also be aware that the written tempos are to be used as a guide. These are the tempos that the accompanying audio files are recorded at, but you should not feel that these are the tempos at which you must start. You should initially study each exercise in free time, with no metronome putting pressure on you to 'understand quickly'. Once you are comfortable with the notes and rhythms you can begin using the metronome, but don't be afraid to start with tempos that are slower than those that are written.

Finally, whilst this book will help you to take your first steps towards reading music fluently, it requires two things from you: commitment, and lots of hard work! Learning to read music is essentially like learning a new language, albeit a relatively simple one. Doing so will require time, daily practice and patience and although it might be frustrating to begin with, the results will be worth it I can assure you.

I hope that you enjoy this book and that it helps you to become a competent reader. As always, I would be delighted to hear your thoughts, and answer any questions that you might have. Please feel free to send emails to stuart@basslinepublishing.com.

Stuart Clayton
January 2013

Chapter 1
The Basics

In this chapter you will be introduced to several basic elements of written music. These include the stave – the framework upon which music is written – the bass clef, time signatures, key signatures and tempo indications. Many of these will be explored in greater detail later in the book, but it is important to be aware of them from this early stage. This chapter will also introduce a basic rhythm and some pitches, meaning that you can start reading some simple music straight away.

The Stave

All music is notated on a **stave**; a series of five horizontal lines onto which the notes are placed. Notes can either be written on lines (meaning that the line goes through the centre of the note head), or between them, as shown in the example below:

Almost all instruments read music from a five-line stave, and you can rest assured that all of the music that you will read as a bass player – and certainly all of the music you will see in this book – will be written on a stave such as the one shown above.

The Bass Clef

Most music that is written for the bass guitar uses the **bass clef**, the curved symbol which appears at the beginning of every line of music. This symbol defines where the notes are situated on the stave. The bass clef is sometimes known as the 'F Clef' because the two dots sit either side of the line that holds the note F:

F

Since this clef shows the location of an F, it is possible to find all of the other notes using this as a reference. In the illustration on the next page, tablature has been used to show the locations of all of the notes on the stave within the first five frets. You can use this illustration as a guide to learning the notes on the stave. Some of these notes will be used in this chapter, whilst others will be introduced in later chapters.

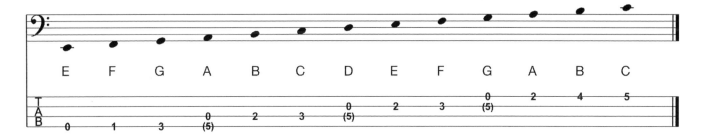

Time Signature

All music is written with a **time signature**, which is written only once, at the very beginning of the piece. A time signature consists of two numbers, one above the other in the form of a fraction. The top number shows the number of beats in a bar, whilst the bottom number indicates the value of those beats. The majority of Western music is written in 4/4 time, meaning that there are four beats in a bar, and the value of those beats is a **quarter note** (or **crotchet**) which is also represented by a number four. Time signatures will be covered in more detail later in the book. For now, you only need to be aware of the basic principle.

TIP!

4/4 time is often referred to as 'common' time, which can be shown using a large, stylised letter C in place of the 4/4 numerals. Whether the C or 4/4 is used, the meaning is the same.

Bars and Bar lines

From the examples given throughout this chapter, you'll see that individual bars are separated by vertical lines. These are known as **bar lines**. The end of a piece is marked by a double bar line – a thin line followed by a thick line. This is only used at the end of a piece of music.

TIP!

In U.S. terminology a bar of music is usually referred to as a 'measure' rather than a bar.

Tempo

All pieces of music should also include a **tempo** indication of some kind. Most tempo indications consist of a note value followed by an equals sign and a number, as shown in the example below.

♩ = 120

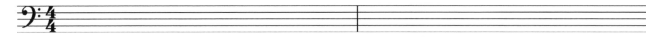

In this example the tempo marking states that the piece is to be played at 120 quarter note beats per minute (quarter notes are covered on the next page). This equates to two beats per second. Different rhythmic values besides quarter notes can of course be used here, but this is the one that you will see most often.

You may also find that the tempo indication is accompanied by a description of the musical style of the piece, such as 'funk rock' or 'bossa nova'. Similarly, words such as 'moderately', or 'slowly' may be used in conjunction with the tempo indication to give a clearer idea of how the piece should sound. Occasionally Italian words such as 'allegro' or 'andante' may be used to describe the piece, but while these terms are commonly found in classical music, they are less common in contemporary pop and rock music. Performance directions such as these will be covered in more detail in the second book of this series.

Key Signatures

A **key signature** is an arrangement of sharps or flats that is written on the stave after the bass clef. The key signature tells the reader which key the piece of music is written in and unlike the time signature, must be written at the beginning of every line of music. Here are two examples of key signatures – one for the key of D major, and one for the key of F major:

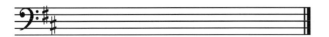

D Major Key Signature

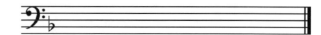

F Major Key Signature

A key signature essentially indicates that certain notes should be played as sharps (or flats) by default. In the first example above – which is the key signature for D major – the key signature shows that all F's and C's should be played as sharpened notes (F♯ and C♯) throughout the piece unless indicated otherwise. In the second example the key signature states that any B's should be played as B♭'s unless indicated otherwise. If you have studied scales, the concept of key signatures will already be familiar. Key signatures will be covered in more detail in Chapter 11.

Quarter Notes /Crotchets

The next element of written music that will be covered here is one of the most basic rhythms – the **quarter note**, or **crotchet**. In 4/4 time, quarter notes last for one beat each, meaning that there can be four of them in a bar. It's important to be aware that the term 'quarter note' is derived from the fact that they last for a quarter of a whole note – we'll be looking at whole notes in the next chapter. As you can see from the example below, quarter notes consist of a black note head and a stem. Rhythmic values are differentiated based on how the notes look – for example, some will have stems, while others won't. Some will be filled black, and others will be empty.

Example 1

♩ = 60

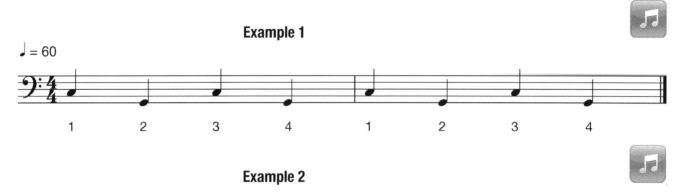

Example 2

If a one beat rest is required, a quarter note rest is written. In this example the rests indicate that nothing is played on beats one and three:

♩ = 60

THE BASS GUITARIST'S GUIDE TO READING MUSIC: BEGINNER

Most contemporary music is counted in quarter notes, and when you are tapping your foot to a piece of music, invariably you will be tapping the quarter note pulse.

TIP!

The traditional English terminology for this note value is crotchet, whereas in countries such as the United States, it is referred to as the quarter note. As the name is more descriptive, the U.S. terminology will be used in this book.

Basic Pitches

The last elements to be covered in this chapter are some basic pitches. The following four notes will be used in the reading exercises at the end of the chapter. These notes are C, G, F and A:

C   G   F   A

You should study the positions of these notes on the stave carefully and try to remember them. You will be able to find these notes on the fretboard of the bass using the illustration on page 7. Note that the F used here is the low F which is found at the first fret of the E-string on the bass. The F that sits between the two dots of the clef is one octave higher than this note and will be used in later chapters.

Chapter Summary

Now that the basics of music notation have been covered in detail, you can begin putting what you have learnt to the test. The following ten exercises feature all of the different elements that have been introduced in this chapter. Each exercise uses only quarter note rhythms and the four basic pitches described above. The last five exercises also incorporate the quarter note rest.

To play these exercises, set a metronome to 60bpm, as indicated at the beginning of each exercise. Tap your foot in time to the metronome clicks – these are the quarter note beats. Count 1, 2, 3, 4, then play. As these exercises use only quarter note rhythms there will be one note on each click. To begin with, you might want to turn off the metronome once you have established the tempo so that you are working on each exercise at your own pace. When you are confident with the notes and rhythms you can try playing with the metronome. Remember that you can also refer to the audio files to ensure you are playing each exercise correctly.

TIP!

If you have never read any music before you will probably find it hard to read these exercises straight away – this is normal. Remember that you should not be afraid to take them a bar at a time, or even a note at a time if you need to. At this early stage you are not expected to sight read these exercises, just learn how to play them by following the music.

EXERCISE 1

This simple exercise has only one different note in each bar.

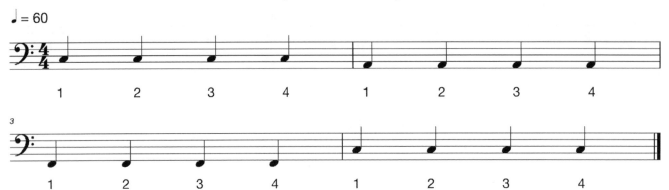

EXERCISE 2

In this exercise, different notes are used in each bar.

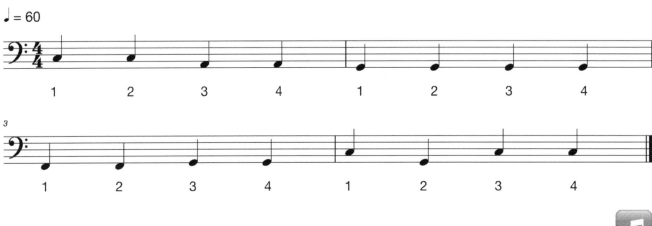

EXERCISE 3

This exercise features a little more variety than the previous two.

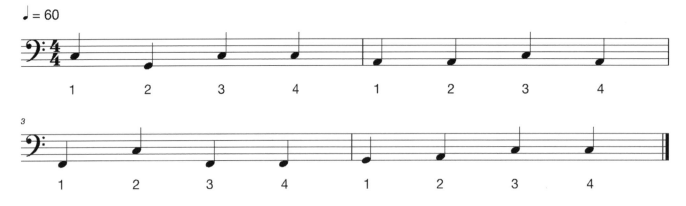

THE BASS GUITARIST'S GUIDE TO READING MUSIC: BEGINNER

EXERCISE 4

EXERCISE 5

This exercise features quite a lot of movement.

EXERCISE 6

This exercise features some quarter note rests on beats 2 and 4. When playing this exercise be careful not to let the notes on beats 1 and 3 ring throughout beats 2 and 4 – there should be silence on those beats. Concentrate on letting the note ring for the full duration of the beat, then having a full beat of silence. Remember that you can refer to the audio track if you need help with playing this exercise.

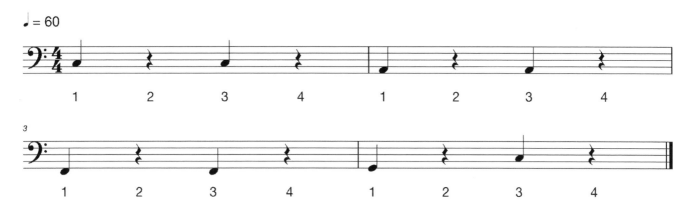

EXERCISE 7

This exercise features a quarter note rest on beat three of each bar.

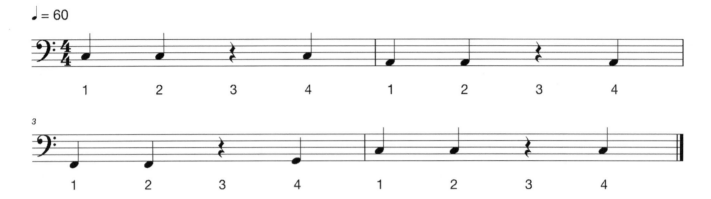

EXERCISE 8

This exercise features more quarter note rests, but with a different rhythmic pattern used in each bar. Take your time with this exercise.

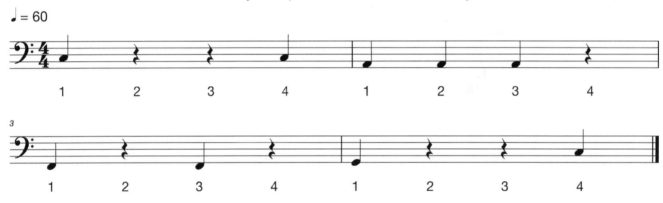

EXERCISE 9

This exercise is tricky because there is a rest on the first beat of the first bar. Be sure to count 'one' here (but don't play!) and play the first note on beat two as written.

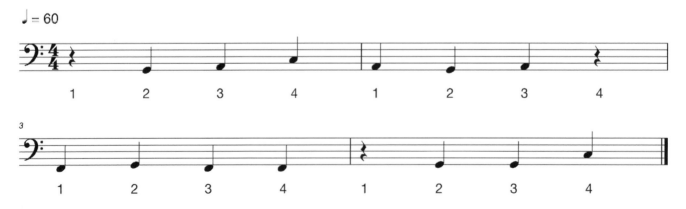

THE BASS GUITARIST'S GUIDE TO READING MUSIC: BEGINNER

EXERCISE 10

This final exercise features a lot of quarter note rests. Count this one carefully.

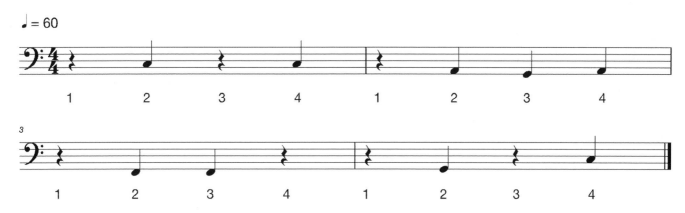

As you work on these exercises you will probably find that you begin to memorise parts of them – this is natural, although it's common for students to worry about this, in the fear that they are not using the reading skills that they are developing. In fact, memorisation is a very natural thing for the brain to do and is an accepted part of sight reading. Although you might find that you are able to memorise large parts of these exercises, this won't be possible as we progress to more complex basslines.

Don't be tempted to move on to the next chapter until you have mastered these ten exercises. Remember that each chapter of this book builds on the previous one, so it's important not to jump ahead too quickly.

Chapter 2

Rhythm

By now you should have a basic understanding of the fundamentals of written music, and you will hopefully have been able to work through the ten exercises at the end of the previous chapter without any serious problems. In this chapter you will be introduced to two new rhythms: the half note and the whole note. You will find that these note values open up more rhythmic possibilities.

Half Note/Minim

The first new rhythm is the **half note**, or **minim**. Half notes are twice as long as the quarter note rhythms that were covered in Chapter 1. Since a half note lasts for two beats, two can be played within a bar of 4/4 time.

Example 1

As you can see, half notes look similar to quarter notes except that their note heads are empty:

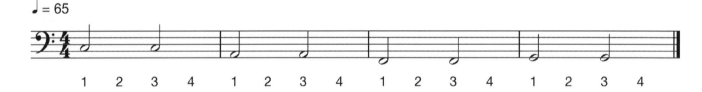

Example 2

In the next example some half note rests have been used. The half note rest is quite unlike the quarter note rest in appearance, and instead looks like a small block sitting on the middle line of the stave:

Before moving on to any further rhythms, it is important to study a few exercises that exclusively use half notes and half note rests. As before, take your time with these and focus on playing each note – or rest – for the correct duration. The same four pitches that were introduced in the previous chapter are used again in these exercises. More notes will be introduced in the next chapter.

THE BASS GUITARIST'S GUIDE TO READING MUSIC: BEGINNER

EXERCISE 11

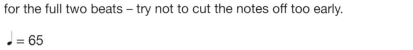

This exercise consists only of half notes. Make sure that each note lasts for the full two beats – try not to cut the notes off too early.

EXERCISE 12

This exercise includes some half note rests. Remember to make sure that the first note in each bar lasts for two **full** beats. As beat three arrives this note should stop and there should be two beats of silence.

EXERCISE 13

This exercise also features a combination of half notes and half note rests, but some of the bars *start* with a rest. Remember to count '1, 2' through these rests and then play on beat three. If in doubt, follow the counting guide below the stave.

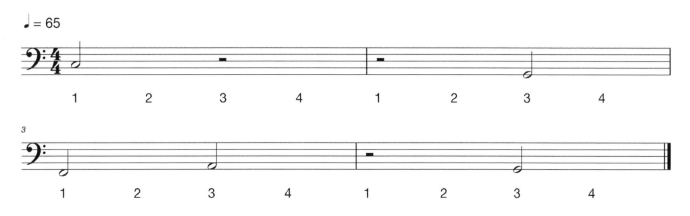

EXERCISE 14

This exercise also features bars which start with a half note rest.

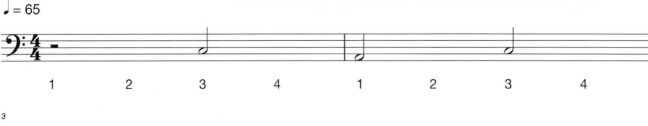

EXERCISE 15

This exercise features another combination of half notes and rests.

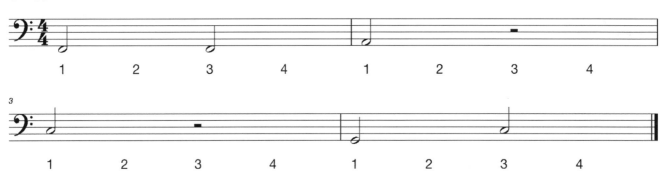

Whole Note/Semibreve

The next rhythmic value that will be covered in this chapter is the **whole note**, or **semibreve**. Whole notes last for four beats each, so as the U.S. terminology suggests, last for a whole bar. As you can see, whole notes look a little different to quarter notes and half notes: they consist only of an empty note head with no stem.

Example 3

Example 4

The next example includes some whole note rests. These look similar to half note rests: a small block, which in this case hangs from the 'F' line of the stave. Be very careful not to confuse this rest with the half note rest.

♩ = 65

| 1 | 2 | 3 | 4 | 1 | 2 | 3 | 4 | 1 | 2 | 3 | 4 | 1 | 2 | 3 | 4 |

Once again, before moving on you should study some exercises that use whole notes. As this rhythm is somewhat limiting there are only two exercises to study here.

EXERCISE 16

This exercise consists solely of whole notes.

♩ = 65

| 1 | 2 | 3 | 4 | 1 | 2 | 3 | 4 | 1 | 2 | 3 | 4 | 1 | 2 | 3 | 4 |

EXERCISE 17

This exercise includes a whole note rest.

♩ = 65

| 1 | 2 | 3 | 4 | 1 | 2 | 3 | 4 | 1 | 2 | 3 | 4 | 1 | 2 | 3 | 4 |

Chapter Summary

In this chapter two new rhythms have been introduced, meaning that from now on there will be more information to digest in each exercise. The following five exercises will combine the half note and whole note with the quarter note rhythm (and rest) from the previous chapter. Remember that a quarter note lasts for one beat, a half note for two, and a whole note for four. Be sure to follow the counting guide below the stave and refer to the audio files for guidance if needed.

EXERCISE 18

This exercise features all of the rhythms covered so far, and no rests.

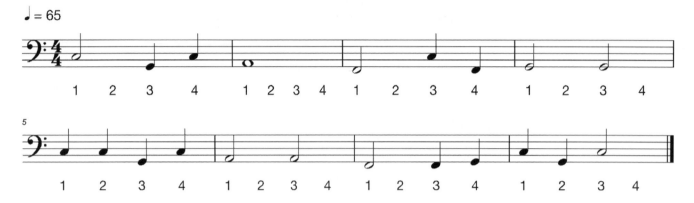

EXERCISE 19

This exercise uses some rests. Remember to not let the notes ring through these.

EXERCISE 20

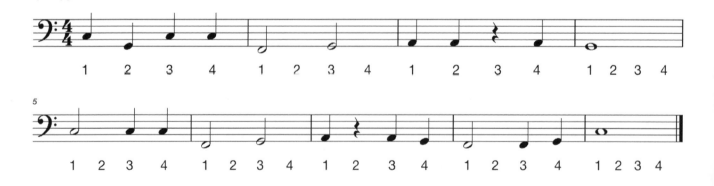

TIP!

As you get better at recognising rhythms and pitches, you may find that you are able to digest the information in one bar quite quickly. If this is the case, try to look ahead while you are playing. As an example, if you are playing a whole note, you will have four beats where you are holding one note – try to use this time to look ahead to what is happening in the next bar. The best sight readers are able to look ahead whilst playing and anticipate any problems in advance.

EXERCISE 21

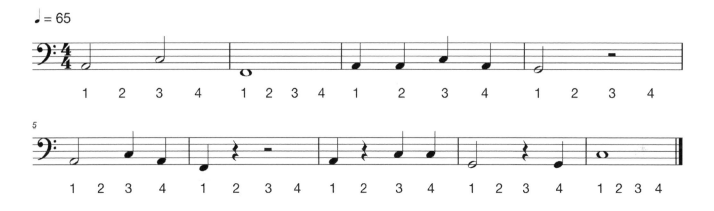

EXERCISE 22

This exercise includes a quarter note rest at the end of the first bar, followed by a whole note rest in the second. Count carefully through this exercise.

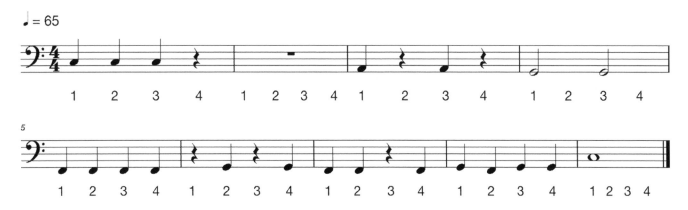

Chapter 3
More Pitches

The last two chapters have introduced many of the basic elements of written music and have given you the opportunity to read some simple exercises. This chapter introduces the three remaining pitches on the stave and has exercises that will allow you to study them alongside the ones that you already know.

The three notes that will be added to the exercises in this chapter are E, B and D:

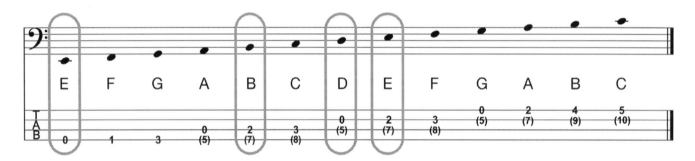

You can see that there are two E's covered here. One is the E that sits in the space below the 'F' line of the bass clef. This E can be found at the second fret of the D-string, or at the seventh fret of the A-string (it can also be found at the twelfth fret of the E-string, although it is less practical to use it in this position for the exercises in this chapter). The other E is the open E-string, which is an octave lower in pitch. You'll see that this note is written on a line added below the stave. These additional lines are known as **ledger lines** and are used when pitches occur above or below the existing stave. As the conventional 4-string bass has E as its lowest note, none of the basslines featured in this book will use notes any lower than this. 5-string basses are capable of producing notes lower than E, and these will be covered in the third book in this series

Each of the other two notes covered in this chapter has two different locations on the fretboard and technically you can use either: the D can either be played at the fifth fret of the A-string or at the open D-string. The B can either be played at the second fret of the A-string, or the seventh fret of the E-string. Although all of the three new notes covered in this chapter are available in several different locations on the fretboard, you will find it easier to play them on the lower frets (or open strings) during the next series of exercises. Doing so will enable you to play all of the notes covered so far within the first five frets of the bass, meaning that you do not need to shift the fretting hand up to the seventh fret for the E or B. Good sight readers will typically play in one position wherever possible as this means that they can concentrate on reading the music rather than worrying about moving their fretting hand around the neck.

Note that exercises from this point on will also make use of the F that is an octave higher than the low F that was used in many of the previous exercises. As you saw in Chapter 1, this higher F is written on the second line down from the top of the stave, which is between the two dots of the bass clef.

TIP!

From now on, when you are given a new piece of music to study, look at the range of notes used – which are the highest and lowest? At this point in the book, the lowest note you will encounter will be the low E and the highest will be the F at the third fret of the D-string. As these notes are found within the first position on the instrument, you should not have to move your fretting hand out of position at all.

Chapter Summary

This chapter has covered the remaining three notes, meaning that there are now seven different pitches to remember: A, B, C, D, E, F and G. Most of them can be found in more than one place on the instrument, and some are used in different octaves. Be sure to study the positions of these notes carefully on the stave – you might find it useful to say the note names aloud as you play them.

EXERCISE 23

EXERCISE 24

EXERCISE 25

EXERCISE 26

EXERCISE 27

EXERCISE 28

♩ = 65

1 2 3 4 1 2 3 4 1 2 3 4 1 2 3 4

1 2 3 4 1 2 3 4 1 2 3 4 1 2 3 4 1 2 3 4

EXERCISE 29

♩ = 65

1 2 3 4 1 2 3 4 1 2 3 4 1 2 3 4

1 2 3 4 1 2 3 4 1 2 3 4 1 2 3 4 1 2 3 4

EXERCISE 30

♩ = 65

1 2 3 4 1 2 3 4 1 2 3 4 1 2 3 4

1 2 3 4 1 2 3 4 1 2 3 4 1 2 3 4 1 2 3 4

EXERCISE 31

EXERCISE 32

TIP!

Several new notes have been introduced in this chapter, and you now have three different rhythmic values (and their respective rests) to contend with. It's very important that you work on the exercises so far thoroughly, only moving on when you are confident that you are able to play all of them by following the notation.

Chapter 4
More Rhythms

This chapter introduces a new rhythm – the eighth note, or quaver. Eighth notes are shorter in duration than any of the other rhythms that have been covered so far and using them will create considerably more variety in the exercises. This will present several new challenges for you in terms of reading.

Eighth Notes/Quavers

Eighth notes – also known as **quavers** – last for half of a beat each, meaning that two can be played per beat. This means that eight eighth notes can be played in one bar. To count eighth notes, you'll now have to count 'and' in between each beat: 1-*and*-2-*and*-3-*and*-4-*and*. Notes that fall on the beat are said to fall on the **downbeat**, whereas notes that fall on the 'and' of the beat fall on the **upbeat**. Eighth notes should be played evenly and should all be equal in length.

As you'll see from the example below, eighth notes look similar to quarter notes in that they have black filled note heads and stems. The difference is that eighth notes also have a 'tail' coming off of the stem.

When several eighth notes are used in succession, their tails are 'beamed' together as shown below. This makes them easier to read.

Note that in the first bar of the example above, the eighth notes have been grouped in pairs. This is the most typical way to beam them together, since it clearly illustrates the four beats in the bar. Beaming in this way makes it clear that two notes are played evenly on each beat. In the second bar, they have been beamed together in groups of four. This can be done for the first and second beats of the bar, and for the third and fourth. One of the rules of notated music is that nothing should cross the centre of the bar – the point between the second and third beats. Therefore, eighth notes would never be beamed together like this:

In the example on the previous page, the centre point of the bar has been shown using a dotted line. In the first bar the line is crossed by beaming from the second beat to the third. The same has happened in the second bar, in which all of the notes have been beamed – eighth notes are never beamed in this way. As you can see from both examples, when incorrect beaming is used, it is difficult to discern the individual beats.

Eighth Note Rests

In this example, eighth note rests are shown. In the first bar, the second half of each beat is silent, so you would effectively play a short note on each beat. In the second bar the *first* part of each beat is silent, and the note falls on the 'and' of each bar, being played on the offbeat.

Note that when eighth notes are used in this way they are often not beamed together.

Common Eighth Note-Based Rhythms

Eighth notes are very important in popular music, and as a bass player you'll play a lot of them! However, before you begin to work on the ten exercises at the end of the chapter, there are a few common eighth note-based rhythms that you should study. All of these are commonly found in popular music, and you should ensure that you are proficient in reading them.

Example 1

This first example is a continuous eighth note bassline and is very commonly used in many genres of music. This rhythm is simple: there are two notes per beat, each of equal value. Be sure to listen to the corresponding audio track as a reference if you are unsure how this rhythm should sound.

Example 2

This example contains quarter notes and eighth notes and is a very commonly used rhythm in popular music. Beat one contains a quarter note, while beat two consists of a rest on the first half of the beat, followed by an eighth note on the upbeat, or 'and' of the beat. This is used once in the first two bars, and twice per bar in the second two bars. This rhythm will probably sound very familiar when you play the third and fourth bars.

♩ = 70

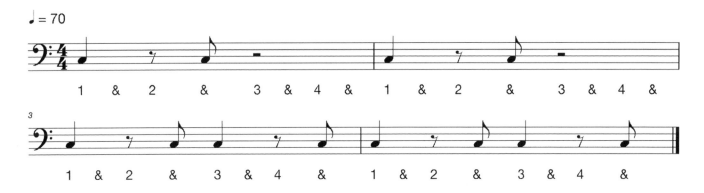

Example 3

This example is similar to Example 2, but this time consists of two eighth notes on beat one, an eighth note rest on beat two, and then another note on the 'and' of beat two. In the example below, this two-beat rhythm is followed by a half note rest in the first two bars, then used two times per bar in the second two bars. Again, you should find that this rhythm sounds quite familiar when you play the third and fourth bars. Remember to refer to the audio or discuss this with your teacher if you need guidance.

♩ = 70

Example 4

This example mixes eighth notes with quarter notes. An eighth is played on beat one, followed by a quarter note on the 'and' of the beat. Since a quarter note lasts for the duration of two eighth notes, this note carries on *into* beat two. This means that the next eighth note is played on the 'and' of beat two. In the example below, this rhythm has been used only once in the first two bars, and twice per bar in the second two bars. Once again, refer to the audio file for guidance if needed.

Chapter Summary

In this chapter a new rhythmic value has been introduced, one that you will find is very commonly used in all styles of music. The next series of exercises will allow you the opportunity to practice reading eighth notes and eighth note rests. You will notice that these exercises are now sixteen bars in length and that the counting guide has been removed.

As before, be sure to work on these exercises slowly, a bar at a time – don't put any pressure on yourself to 'sight-read' them. Remember that at this stage you are still absorbing the language of notated music, and more fluent reading will come once you are completely comfortable with that language.

EXERCISE 33

This exercise features a continuous eighth note bassline. Whilst it looks quite complex, it is simpler to play than it looks: many of the bars only contain one pitch, meaning that you can focus solely on playing the notes evenly. Some of the bars in the second half of the exercise do feature different pitches however, so watch out for those.

EXERCISE 34

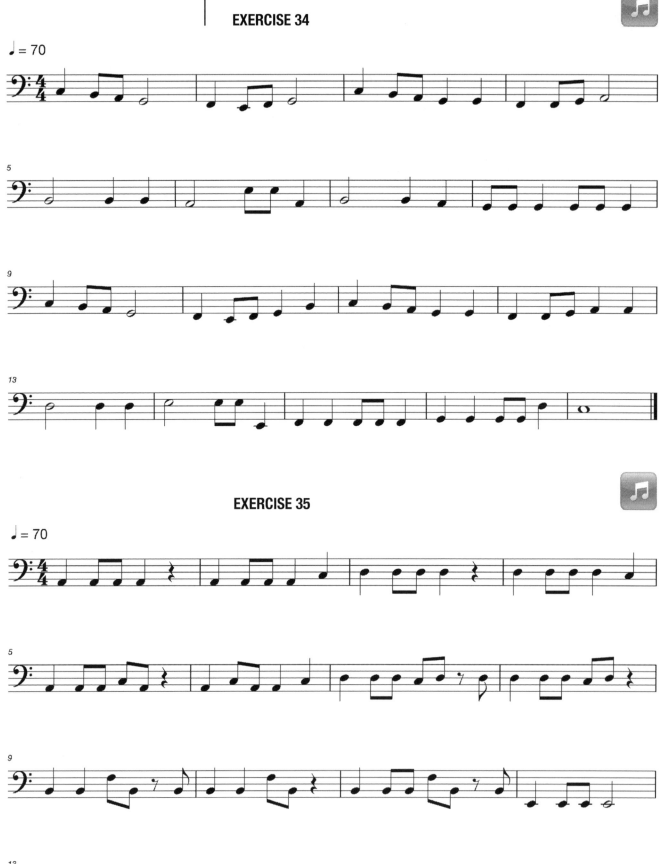

EXERCISE 35

EXERCISE 36

♩ = 70

EXERCISE 37

♩ = 70

EXERCISE 38

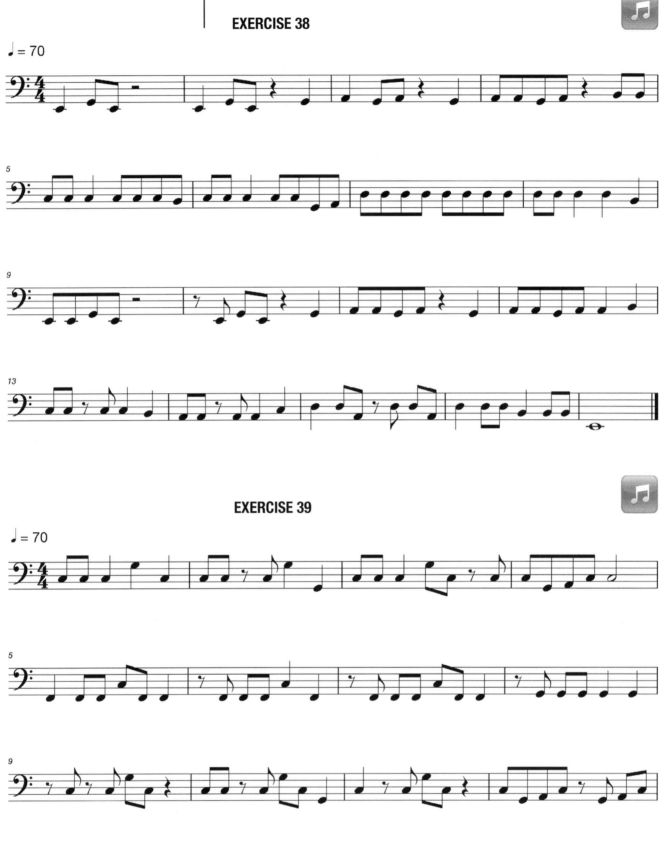

EXERCISE 39

THE BASS GUITARIST'S GUIDE TO READING MUSIC: BEGINNER

EXERCISE 40

♩ = 70

EXERCISE 41

♩ = 70

EXERCISE 42

THE BASS GUITARIST'S GUIDE TO READING MUSIC: BEGINNER

Chapter 5

Octaves

This chapter will cover octaves for all of the notes that have been covered so far. As you will no doubt be aware already, octaves are an important tool for bass players and it's crucial to be able to recognise and read them on the stave. This chapter is also the first of a series of chapters that will look at different intervals on the stave and will feature exercises that specifically focus on developing the ability to recognise and read those intervals.

So far in the book we have covered all of the natural notes, two of which (E and F) have already been used in different octaves. This chapter will focus on octaves of all of the other notes. As some of these will be written above the top line of the stave, some ledger lines will need to be used to notate these. In the illustration below, you can see all of the natural notes up to the G at the twelfth fret of the G-string, together with all of their possible positions on the fretboard:

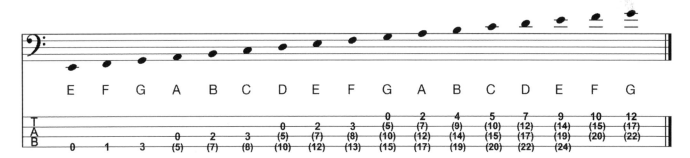

TIP!

You should already be familiar with the notes on the fingerboard of the bass guitar – if not, it is recommended that you make learning these a priority. At this point, not knowing all of the possible locations of all of the notes on the fingerboard is going to seriously hinder your progress with reading music.

Recognising Octaves

Octaves are an extremely common interval in basslines from all genres, and it's important to be able to recognise them on the stave quickly. A big part of being a fluent sight reader is the ability to recognise intervals – being able to do so means that your brain does not necessarily have to think about reading the octave note, it just 'sees' that the note is an octave higher than the previous one. Since octaves naturally fall under the fingers, they can be played easily. Let's look at the octave on the stave and consider how it looks:

Octave with root note in a space

Octave with root note on a line

As you can see, an octave sits either three lines plus a space above the root, or three spaces plus a line above, depending on the location of the root note. This is a large interval and will be difficult to recognise at first. After studying the ten exercises that follow you will hopefully have begun to see it. This will be reinforced in the fact that many of the exercises that you see in this book from now on will feature octaves. You will find that now that octaves are used you will need to move your fretting hand around the neck more – you will not always be able to play these exercises in one hand position.

Chapter Summary

This chapter has been brief but has introduced you to a lot of new notes on the stave and the first important interval to recognise. Practice the following exercises carefully and only move on once you are confident you have completed them all to a high standard.

EXERCISE 43

EXERCISE 44

EXERCISE 45

EXERCISE 46

THE BASS GUITARIST'S GUIDE TO READING MUSIC: BEGINNER

EXERCISE 48

EXERCISE 49

EXERCISE 50

EXERCISE 51

EXERCISE 52

Chapter 6
Ties and Dotted Rhythms

This chapter will focus on two rhythmic devices that allow notes to be extended in ways that have not been possible so far. For example, in some situations a note may be required to last for three beats, for longer than a bar, or for a beat and a half. These rhythms cannot be written with quarter notes and half notes alone, but you will find that by using dotted notes or ties, these and many other potential note durations are possible.

Ties

The first new rhythmic device that this chapter will cover is the **tie**. A tie is a curved line that connects two notes. When two (or more) notes are tied, only the first is played, but it lasts for the duration of all of the tied notes. The following examples will illustrate the use of ties.

Example 1

In this first example a half note has been tied to a quarter note to create a note that lasts for three beats:

Example 2

In this example a quarter note has been tied to an eighth note, creating a note which lasts for a beat and a half. The first note lasts for all of the first beat and the first half of the second. The second is then played on the upbeat, or 'and' of beat two:

TIP!

Note that this example is very similar to Example 2 of Chapter 4, which consisted of a quarter note on beat one, an eighth note rest on the downbeat of beat two, and an eighth note on the upbeat of beat two. The placement of the notes in this example is identical, the difference being that when the notes are tied, the first note lasts until the second note is played. In the example from Chapter 4, the first note only lasts until beat two, and then stops where the rest is written at the beginning of the beat.

Example 3

In this example, a whole note has been tied to the first quarter note in the following bar. The first note is therefore held throughout the first bar and the first beat of the second. The next note is played on the second beat of the second bar:

Example 4

Finally, you should be aware that ties are written beneath the notes if the stems are pointing upwards and above the notes if the stems are pointing downwards:

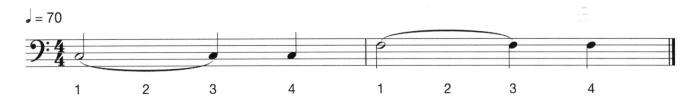

That's really all there is to know about ties. You will of course have the chance to work on exercises that make use of them at the end of this chapter.

Dotted Notes

The second rhythmic device that will be covered in this chapter is the **dotted note**. Like ties, dotted notes are used to extend the duration of a rhythm. When placed after a note, a dot extends its value by 50%. Here are a few examples of dotted notes in action.

Example 5

In this example a dot has been added to a half note, meaning that it will now last for *three* beats instead of two:

Example 6

In this example a dot has been added to a quarter note, meaning that it now lasts for a beat and a half. The second note is therefore played on the 'and' of beat two.

TIP!

This is essentially the same rhythm as the second tie example from earlier in the chapter. Whilst either is acceptable, dotted notes are more commonly used in this scenario. This rhythm is very common in basslines from all genres.

Example 7

This rhythm can also be written the other way around: an eighth note followed by a dotted quarter note:

You can also add a dot after an eighth note. This will result in a note that lasts for *three quarters* of a beat instead of half a beat. This rhythm will be covered in the *Advanced Level* book of this series.

Chapter Summary

This chapter has introduced two new elements that will have a significant impact on the scope of the rhythms which are now possible. You should take your time when studying the following exercises – these basslines are quite complex in places. When learning them you might find it helps to write the beats beneath the stave in order to see which part of the beat the notes are falling on. Finally, remember that you are not expected to sight read these exercises, but to **learn** them from studying the notation. You can use the downloadable audio files for reference if needed, but I would recommend that you do as much as you can just with a metronome. As stated at the beginning of this book, working on this material with a good teacher will also be very beneficial to you.

The first three exercises feature the use of ties and the following three feature dotted rhythms. The final four exercises will use a combination of both.

EXERCISE 53

♩ = 70

EXERCISE 54

EXERCISE 55

EXERCISE 56

♩ = 70

EXERCISE 57

♩ = 70

EXERCISE 58

♩ = 70

EXERCISE 59

♩ = 70

THE BASS GUITARIST'S GUIDE TO READING MUSIC: BEGINNER

EXERCISE 60

EXERCISE 61

EXERCISE 62

THE BASS GUITARIST'S GUIDE TO READING MUSIC: BEGINNER

Chapter 7
Navigation

This chapter will introduce you to many of the navigation symbols that are commonly found in printed music. These include symbols for repeating sections of music – whether it be one bar or several – and symbols for returning to earlier sections of a piece or jumping to later sections.

Repeat Sections

The first elements of navigation that will be covered here are **repeat bar lines**. These can be seen below and consist of a double bar line, with two dots either side of the line that holds the note D. These are placed at either end of the section of music that is to be repeated.

Example 1

In the example below, the last two bars are encompassed by repeat markings, and so should be played through **twice**. After repeating these bars, you would carry on reading through the piece as normal.

Example 2

Sometimes you will be required to repeat a section *more* than once. When this happens, a performance direction such as 'play 3x' will be indicated above or below the repeated section. In this example, you would play the last two bars **three** times in total before moving on.

Example 3

When the music requires you to repeat back to the *beginning* of the piece, the first repeat marking will not be written, as shown below:

Example 4

Sometimes a section will be written with repeat markings, but with different endings required each time, as shown below. In this scenario, you would play through the first three bars as normal, then play the first time ending (the bracketed section labelled 1.). You would then return to the beginning of the piece as directed by the repeat bar line – note that there is not a start repeat mark here as the repeat goes back to the beginning of the piece. On the second time through, the first time ending would be **ignored** and the second would be played.

This example would therefore be played as follows:

As many different endings as needed can be written using this method, although it is most common to see just two.

Repeat Bar Symbols

There are also symbols that allow for just one bar of music to be repeated. The repeat bar symbol (shown below) is often used to save having to write out the same bar of music repeatedly.

Example 5

In this example, the music from the first bar is played again in the second, third and fourth bars. This symbol is commonly used in many genres of music and you are likely to encounter it often.

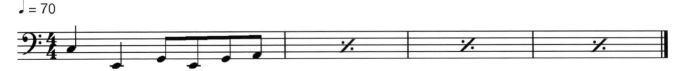

Example 6

A similar symbol – with two diagonal lines instead of one – can be used to show that **two** bars of music are to be played again:

The above example could also have been notated using repeat bar lines.

Example 7

Finally, a similar symbol with four diagonal lines can be used to indicate that the previous **four** bars should be played again:

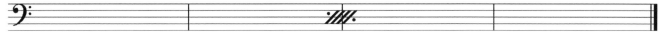

This symbol is less common than the one and two bar repeat symbols.

> **TIP!**
>
> The two and four bar repeat symbols are sometimes shown with the corresponding numbers 2 and 4 written above them to clarify exactly how many bars are to be repeated.

Signs and Codas

The final elements of navigation that will be covered in this chapter are the **Sign** and the **Coda**. These devices are used in longer pieces of music in situations where an earlier section is to be played again. This section may, on longer pieces, be a whole page or more back in the score. Rather than write the part out again, making the score even longer, composers use Signs and Codas to show that a previous section is to be repeated.

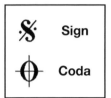

Sign

Coda

The first direction that you are likely to see is **Dal Segno al Coda**, which is often abbreviated to **D.S al Coda**. The first part of this statement, 'Dal Segno', is Italian for 'from the Sign' and tells the reader to go back to the earlier section that begins with the Sign symbol. The second part of the direction 'al Coda' states that after going back to the Sign, you should then play through to the point in the music where it says 'al Coda' or more commonly, 'to Coda'. The Coda is the final section of a piece of music, so at this point you would jump to the end section of the piece, marked with the Coda symbol.

Example 8

This example illustrates both the Coda and Sign in use. When playing this piece you would therefore play through until the end of bar 12, where you would then follow the direction to go back to the Sign, which is at the beginning of bar 5. You would then play from bar 5 to the end of bar 8, at which point you would follow the direction to go to the Coda, which begins at bar 13. You would then play from this point to the end of the piece.

An alternative direction that you will sometimes see is **Da Capo al Coda**, sometimes abbreviated to **D.C al Coda**. This is another Italian phrase meaning 'from the head', or 'from the beginning'. When you see this direction, you should go back to the very beginning of the piece, then play until you see the words 'al Coda', or 'To Coda'. At this point, you would jump to the Coda.

THE BASS GUITARIST'S GUIDE TO READING MUSIC: BEGINNER

Example 9

In this example, you would play through the piece until the direction **D.C al Coda** at the end of bar 12. At this point you would return to the beginning of the piece, play through until the end of bar 8, then jump to the Coda at bar 13 and then play to the end.

Example 10

A final variation on these phrases would be to replace 'al Coda' with 'al Fine', which is another Italian phrase, meaning 'the end'. Therefore, when following the phrase **Da Capo al Fine** you would return to the beginning of the piece and then play until the word 'Fine'. At this point you would stop as this would be the end of the piece:

TIP!

Note that in the example on the previous page the word 'Fine' is ignored the first time around. This word is only relevant after following a 'Da Capo' or 'Dal Segno' direction.

Chapter Summary

In this chapter we have covered a range of navigation markings, all of which are very common in popular music. You will encounter all of these devices on a regular basis as a reading bass player, so it's important to become as familiar with them as possible. There will be a selection of exercises at the end of this first section of the book that put some of these devices to use.

Chapter 8
Time Signatures

So far all of the exercises in this book have been written in 4/4 time, which is representative of much of the notated music that you will encounter as a bass player. However, there will be instances where other time signatures are required, and it is important for you to be fluent at reading in all of them. You'll be pleased to know that all of the rhythmic elements that have been covered so far still apply, so learning a new time signature should not prove as challenging as you might think.

Time signatures fall into three categories: **simple**, **compound** and **irregular**. Simple time signatures have 4 as the beat unit (the lower number), meaning that in each, one beat is equal to a quarter note. Examples of this include 4/4 (which has already been used in every exercise so far), 2/4 (which is essentially just half of a bar of 4/4), and 3/4. Compound time signatures have 8 as their beat unit, although in this case the 8 does not equate to the value of the beats in a bar (compound time signatures will be covered in the next book in this series). Irregular time signatures can contain either 4, 8 or 16 as the lower number, but feature uneven numbers of beats in each bar. These will be covered in the third book. This chapter will focus on 3/4, a simple time signature.

3/4 Time

3/4 time is quite commonly used in popular music and is definitely a time signature that you should become comfortable reading. Pieces of music written in 3/4 are typically referred to as 'waltzes' and although this may seem like an old-fashioned term, there are many examples of waltzes in pop music. Some good examples of songs in 3/4 include: 'Mull of Kintyre' by Paul McCartney, 'Lucy in the Sky with Diamonds' (Verse section) by The Beatles, 'Piano Man' by Billy Joel, 'Manic Depression' by Jimi Hendrix and 'Blackout' by Muse.

Example 1

In 3/4 time there are three crochet beats in a bar:

In terms of reading music in 3/4 time, there is little real difference to reading music in 4/4 time! You will however notice that having only three beats in a bar gives the music a very different feel. The following five exercises will allow you the opportunity to read some music in 3/4. The beat count has been written underneath these exercises as a guide. Remember to work on these in free time initially, referring to the audio tracks to check for accuracy.

Chapter Summary

This chapter has introduced a new time signature, one that you are sure to encounter in your career as a reading bass player. Hopefully the process of studying this time signature and the five exercises that follow will demonstrate that different time signatures are often not particularly complex. Any time signature with a beat unit of four – 2/4, 5/4, 7/4 for example – is still played with the same quarter note count, just with a different number of beats in each bar. The number of beats in a bar affects the feel of the music enormously, but hopefully you can see that the principles of reading music written in these time signatures remain the same.

EXERCISE 63

THE BASS GUITARIST'S GUIDE TO READING MUSIC: BEGINNER

EXERCISE 64

♩ = 85

EXERCISE 65

♩ = 85

EXERCISE 66

EXERCISE 67

THE BASS GUITARIST'S GUIDE TO READING MUSIC: BEGINNER

Chapter 9
Thirds

This chapter is similar to Chapter 5 in that it focuses solely on one interval. In Chapter 5 the octave – a wide interval – was examined in detail and by now you will hopefully have played several exercises that make use of it. With a bit of luck, you will also be starting to recognise it when you see it used in written music. In this chapter we are going to focus on a much smaller interval, the third.

If you are familiar with music theory, you will be aware that thirds come in two varieties, the **major third** and the **minor third**. Regardless of whether they are major or minor however, thirds have a very recognisable appearance on the stave:

Major Third

Minor Third

As you can see, thirds always appear on adjacent lines or in adjacent spaces. This is most obvious in the second bar of each example where the notes have been stacked on top of each other to demonstrate their appearance on the stave more clearly. When notes are stacked vertically in this way they would be played together. This is how chords are written on the stave, although technically, a chord containing only two notes is referred to as a **double stop**.

In the example above, the first third is a major third because the two notes are C and E – these notes are separated by **four** half steps (or semitones), which is instead described as a **major third**.

C	C♯	D	D♯	E
	1	2	3	4

The second third however is a minor third, as the two notes are D and F. These notes are separated by **three** half steps, which are equal to a **minor third**.

D	D♯	E	F
	1	2	3

The type of third will depend on which key you are in and whether any accidentals are being used (accidentals will be covered in the next chapter).

TIP!

For more information on thirds, or indeed any other interval, check out Chapters 8 and 9 of *The Bass Guitarist's Guide to Scales & Modes*, also available from Bassline Publishing.

It is a good idea to be familiar with the fretboard shape for each of these intervals. These are demonstrated below:

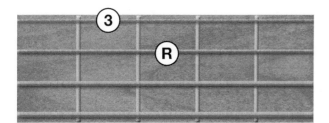

Major Third

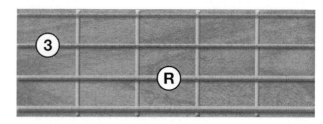

Minor Third

As you can see, if your second finger were to be fretting a root note (marked with an 'R'), the major third would be playable with the first finger, on the next string and back one fret. Similarly, fretting a note with the third finger (using the second would be a bit of a stretch) you would be able to play the note that is a minor third higher with the first finger on the next string and two frets back.

It's also a good idea to be able to play thirds on one string, as shown in the diagrams below:

Major Third on one string

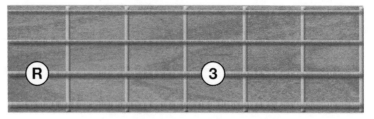

Minor Third on one string

As you can see, when played on one string the minor third interval falls quite neatly under the fingers (with the first finger on the root and the fourth on the minor third), whereas the major third is more of a stretch and is beyond the finger-per-fret reach.

The point of being able to recognise thirds (or any interval) on the stave is that it can be enormously beneficial when reading. Experienced sight readers will notice that the interval between two notes is a third, then taking into consideration the key they are in, will automatically be able to play it without necessarily thinking about its pitch. Be aware however that this level of intervallic sight reading comes with years of experience and you should not put any pressure on yourself to read in this way initially.

Chapter Summary

In this chapter we have covered one of the most important intervals in music – the third. This is a small interval and is possibly the easiest to recognise on the stave. The exercises that follow will allow you to practice reading basslines that use thirds extensively.

EXERCISE 68

EXERCISE 69

EXERCISE 70

THE BASS GUITARIST'S GUIDE TO READING MUSIC: BEGINNER

EXERCISE 71

♩ = 80

EXERCISE 72

♩ = 80

THE BASS GUITARIST'S GUIDE TO READING MUSIC: BEGINNER

EXERCISE 73

EXERCISE 74

THE BASS GUITARIST'S GUIDE TO READING MUSIC: BEGINNER

EXERCISE 75

♩ = 80

EXERCISE 76

♩ = 80

EXERCISE 77

THE BASS GUITARIST'S GUIDE TO READING MUSIC: BEGINNER

Chapter 10
Accidentals

So far in this book all of the pieces of music that you have read have been in the key of C and as such, there have been no sharpened or flattened notes. New keys will be introduced in the next chapter, and in preparation for that, this chapter introduces accidentals.

An **accidental** is a note which **does not belong to the key**. For example, in a piece of the music written in the key of C (which contains only natural notes) any note that is sharpened or flattened would be an accidental. There are a few rules that should be adhered to when reading and writing accidentals, and these are detailed here.

Example 1

The most important thing to understand initially is that an accidental applies for the remainder of the bar in which it is written. So, in the example below, all of the remaining F's within the bar would be played as F#'s – the sharp sign does not need to be added to each one individually.

Example 2

However, if F's were required after the F#, a **natural** sign would be used. This would then cancel out the sharp sign that was added earlier:

Example 3

The next important fact to be aware of is that an accidental only applies in the stave position where it is written. Therefore, in the next example, which uses octaves, a sharp sign is also needed before the higher note:

Example 4

If a note written with an accidental is tied into the following bar, the accidental does not need to be written again for the tied note. However, if the sharpened note is required *after* the tied note, the accidental must be used again as shown below:

F# _

Example 5

Accidentals only apply to the bar in which they are written. So, in the example below, the F's in the second bar are once again F naturals:

F# _ _ _ _ _ _ _ _ _ _ _ _ _ _ _   F _ _ _ _ _ _ _

However, you should be aware that in some instances a natural sign will be added in the second bar just to be sure that the reader reverts back to the correct note.

F# _ _ _ _ _ _ _ _ _ _ _ _ _ _ _   F _ _ _ _ _ _ _

It is not strictly necessary to do this, but it is quite common to see.

Chapter Summary

This chapter has demonstrated the conventions for using accidentals in notation, an important concept to grasp when learning to read. The ten exercises that follow will allow you to put what you have learnt in this chapter to the test. You will probably notice that these exercises are a little more complex than those featured in earlier chapters. Whilst they may take a little longer to learn, there is nothing here that has not been covered in detail in the book so far.

THE BASS GUITARIST'S GUIDE TO READING MUSIC: BEGINNER

EXERCISE 78

EXERCISE 79

EXERCISE 80

EXERCISE 81

THE BASS GUITARIST'S GUIDE TO READING MUSIC: BEGINNER

EXERCISE 82

♩ = 80

EXERCISE 83

♩ = 80

EXERCISE 84

EXERCISE 85

EXERCISE 86

♩ = 80

EXERCISE 87

♩ = 80

Chapter 11

Key Signatures

This chapter covers key signatures, the arrangements of sharps or flats that are usually included at the beginning of each line of music. Key signatures are used to tell the reader what key a piece of music is in and mean that fewer accidentals need to be written. In this chapter you will be introduced to the first four key signatures – those that include up to two sharps and those that include up to two flats. The exercises at the end of this chapter will give you the opportunity to read music that puts these key signatures to use.

If you know anything about scales, you will be aware that most keys contain sharpened or flattened notes by default. The only key that contains neither is C major, which consists of only natural notes. Because of this, when you see a piece of music written with no key signature, it is likely that it is written in the key of C major:

C Major Scale

C Major Key Signature

However, all other keys contain at least one sharpened or flattened note. To save having to continuously write sharp or flat symbols throughout a piece (and more importantly, to make it easier to read), a **key signature** is used to indicate that certain notes are to be played sharp/flat by default.

Sharp Keys

The first key signature that will be covered here is the key signature for the key of G major. This key is the most logical key to learn after C major, as it contains only one sharp – F♯:

G Major Scale

G Major Key Signature

As you may already be aware, every major scale has a **relative minor key** which contains the same notes. For example, the keys of C major and A minor are related as they each contain only the natural notes. G major and E minor are related as each contain only one sharp, F♯. Related keys share the same key signature, so be aware that if you see a key signature with just an F♯, the key could be either G major or E minor.

You can find the relative minor key of a major key by simply counting up six degrees of the major scale:

G	A	B	C	D	E	F♯	G
1	2	3	4	5	6	7	8

THE BASS GUITARIST'S GUIDE TO READING MUSIC: BEGINNER

TIP!

For a full breakdown of all major/minor keys see *The Bass Guitarist's Guide to Scales & Modes*, also available from Bassline Publishing.

The next key signature contains two sharps – F♯ and C♯ – and is the key of D major. You might have noticed that the new sharp that is added to each new scale is the sharpened seventh of the scale, or **leading note**. This is a good way to determine the key when looking at a key signature containing sharps: simply look at the last sharp that is written and count up a half step.

D Major Scale

D Major Key Signature

If you count up six degrees of the D major scale you will see that the relative minor key is B minor. Therefore, a key signature with two sharps tells us that the key is either D major or B minor.

The keys of G and D major are the only two sharp keys that will be covered in this book. You will have the chance to read music written in these keys at the end of this chapter.

Flat Keys

The first flat key that will be covered here is the key of F major, which contains only one flat – a B♭.

F Major Scale

F Major Key Signature

Counting up to the sixth degree of the F major scale will show you that this key signature also applies to the key of D minor.

The second flat key signature that will be covered in this chapter is the key of B♭, which has two flats:

B♭ Major Scale

B♭ Major Key Signature

When studying a flat key signature, the key can be determined by looking at the second to last flat written. In the case of B♭ major, the second to last flat is B♭ (it's also the first flat written in this case), and this tells you the major key. This key signature also applies to the key of G minor.

When studying the exercises at the end of this chapter you will see that the use of key signatures means that there are fewer accidentals to read. This makes the score less cluttered and therefore easier to read. To illustrate this further, the following bassline – which is in the key of F♯ major – has been written with and without a key signature, clearly illustrating the difference.

Example 1

No key signature has been used in this example, meaning that all of the required sharps have to be written:

♩ = 100

Example 2

In this example the appropriate key signature has been used, cleaning up the score nicely and making it a lot easier to read.

♩ = 100

Chapter Summary

This chapter has introduced you to the concept of key signatures. The following ten exercises have been written using the key signatures covered in this chapter, so you'll need to study them carefully before you start playing. Whilst this might be difficult at first, with practice and repetition you will begin to recognise key signatures and will learn to automatically sharpen or flatten notes as needed.

EXERCISE 88

This exercise has a key signature of just one sharp and so is in the key of G major.

♩ = 90

5

9

13

THE BASS GUITARIST'S GUIDE TO READING MUSIC: BEGINNER

EXERCISE 89

This exercise has the same key signature as the previous one but is in the relative minor key – E minor.

♩ = 80

EXERCISE 90

This exercise has a key signature of two sharps and is in the key of D major.

♩ = 80

EXERCISE 91

This exercise has a key signature with one flat, so is in the key of F major.

EXERCISE 92

This exercise also has a key signature of one flat but is in the relative minor key of D minor.

THE BASS GUITARIST'S GUIDE TO READING MUSIC: BEGINNER

EXERCISE 93

This exercise is in the key of G major.

♩ = 85

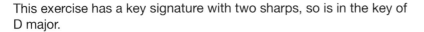

EXERCISE 94

This exercise has a key signature with two sharps, so is in the key of D major.

♩ = 85

EXERCISE 95

This exercise has a key signature with one flat, so is in the key of F major. This bassline continuously moves between two chords and features some tricky syncopated lines.

EXERCISE 96

This exercise is in the key of G minor.

EXERCISE 97

This exercise is a 12-bar blues in D major.

Beginner Level
Exercise Area

This final chapter of the first book is where everything that has been covered so far comes together. The ten extended exercises included here will give you the opportunity to put everything you have learnt to the test.

This book has covered many of the fundamentals of written music in extensive detail. Hopefully, through studying the exercises presented in each chapter, you are now familiar with the basic principles of reading: time signatures, basic rhythms, dotted and tied notes, navigation, accidentals, and the importance of learning to recognise intervals on the stave.

The ten exercises presented here are longer and a little more complex than those featured in this book so far. They are also 'real world' exercises in that they are written in a particular style i.e. funk, ballad, pop etc. Consequently, the chords played by the backing instruments have been written above the stave (as they would be in most real scores) and the backing tracks are full instrumental tracks rather than just a metronome. This should give you a feel for how the elements of written music that have been covered so far work in the context of actual pieces of music. Note that there are two audio files for each exercise – one which includes the recorded bassline for reference, and one without bass for you to use as a backing track.

As I have stated several times throughout the book already, you should not put pressure on yourself to sight read these exercises. Instead you should study each one in detail, learning to play them at your own pace by working with the notation. Of course, you can use the audio files as a reference, but hopefully by now you will be starting to become comfortable with learning to play a simple piece of music from notation.

At this point it is a good idea to consider the best approach to reading a new piece of music. An experienced musician would consider the following four questions before playing anything:

1. What key is the piece in? Obviously this will be determined by the key signature, but remember that each key signature can relate to either a major key, or its relative minor key. Key signatures of up to two sharps or two flats will be used here.

2. What is the time signature? Usually this will be 4/4, but not always. You should also look at the tempo at the beginning of the piece as well. Faster tempos are usually more challenging.

3. Are there any navigation directions to consider? Look out for repeat marks or Coda/Sign directions, and make sure you understand where they go.

4. Are there any particularly difficult parts? Look out for sections that look challenging. It's a good idea to go over any rhythms you find difficult, or pitches you can't remember before you start working on the exercise with your instrument.

It is recommended that you consider these four questions every time you look at a new piece of music, whether it is a complete song, or just an exercise.

EXERCISE 98

This exercise is a ballad. The bassline is built on the dotted quarter note – eighth note idea that was introduced back in Chapter 6. This is a very commonly used rhythm when playing a ballad and this exercise should demonstrate how suitable it is. Note that this exercise also includes some rehearsal marks – an A section and a B section etc. These are used to indicate different sections of a piece, and you can think of them in the same way as you might think of a Verse or a Chorus. There are also some Coda directions to consider, as well as a repeated section at the beginning of the piece with first and second time bar endings. You should refer to Chapter 7 for guidance on these elements if needed.

TIP!

Don't be put off by all of the extra symbols that have suddenly appeared on the page. Although chord symbols and rehearsal marks have not been covered in this book, they are written here merely to demonstrate elements of notated music that you will commonly see. You should still focus your attention on the pitches, rhythm and navigation as you have been doing throughout the book so far.

EXERCISE 99

This exercise is a bossa nova, which is a simple Latin feel. The dotted quarter note-eighth note rhythm is used extensively again here. This is a commonly used rhythm in bossa nova grooves.

THE BASS GUITARIST'S GUIDE TO READING MUSIC: BEGINNER

EXERCISE 100

This exercise is a Motown-style bassline. Motown lines tend to be quite rhythmically complex and this exercise features some tricky syncopated parts. I recommend that you focus on mastering the rhythm in the first two bars. The tricky syncopation in bar 2 is very common in Motown and is reused several times throughout this exercise.

TIP!

The term 'syncopation' means 'a shift of accent in a passage that occurs when a normally weak beat – or part of a beat – is stressed'. In exercises such as the one above, there are many notes that are played on offbeats. Passages such as these (bar 2 is an example) are said to be syncopated.

EXERCISE 101

This exercise is a waltz, and is written at a tempo of 100bpm, which is faster than most of the exercises in this book so far. Fortunately, the bassline here consists largely of quarter notes with a few eighth notes added in sporadically. The challenge here is position playing: you'll need to start on the D at the fifth fret of the A-string in order to play the octave D in the second bar. You'll find that much of the exercise can be played in one position, but there are a couple of places where you will need to shift. Remember to look through the music carefully before starting to read it so that you can see where the position shifts are needed. Watch out for the repeat at the end as well…!

THE BASS GUITARIST'S GUIDE TO READING MUSIC: BEGINNER

EXERCISE 102

This exercise is a rock and roll bassline built predominantly from continuous eighth notes. This line is a great exercise for working on recognising thirds on the stave.

Rock & Roll ♩ = 100

EXERCISE 103

This exercise is a metal bassline that is based on an eighth note feel. You should read each bar carefully: whilst many appear to be repeats of previous bars, in some cases there are subtle differences.

> **TIP!**
>
> There are more chord symbols in use here, including one that has not been used yet: N.C. This simply means that there is no chord played at this point as the guitar is doubling the riff played by the bass.

THE BASS GUITARIST'S GUIDE TO READING MUSIC: BEGINNER

EXERCISE 104

This exercise is a pop reggae bassline and consists only of eighth notes and eighth note rests.

EXERCISE 105

This exercise is a walking bassline over a common set of jazz chord changes. This line only features quarter notes, but contains a few sharps and flats, making it the perfect exercise to use to practice reading accidentals.

continued...

THE BASS GUITARIST'S GUIDE TO READING MUSIC: BEGINNER

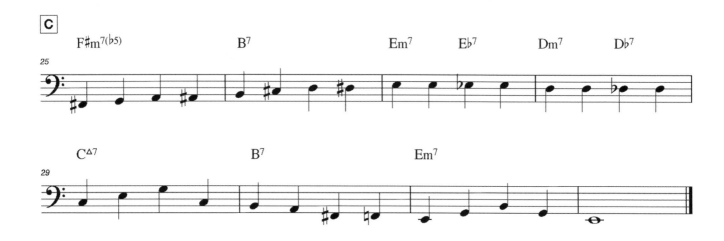

EXERCISE 106

This exercise is a disco bassline that includes a lot of accidentals.
There are also some repeat markings for you to follow.

EXERCISE 107

This final exercise is a rock bassline that is based on an eighth note feel.

THE BASS GUITARIST'S GUIDE TO READING MUSIC: BEGINNER

Bassline Publishing Transcription Books

The following transcription books are available from Bassline Publishing

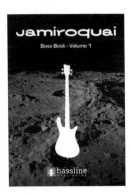

The Jamiroquai Bass
Book - Volume 1

The Jamiroquai Bass
Book - Volume 2

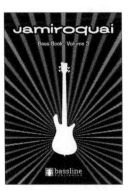

The Jamiroquai Bass
Book - Volume 3

The Jamiroquai Bass
Book - Volume 4

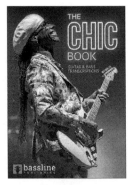

The Chic Book - Guitar
& Bass Transcriptions

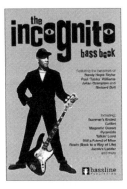

The Incognito
Bass Book

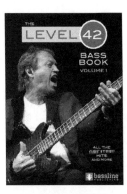

The Level 42 Bass
Book - Volume 1

The Level 42 Bass
Book - Volume 2

The Level 42 Bass
Book - Volume 3

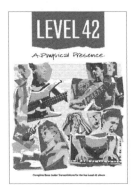

Level 42 -
A Physical Presence

The Mark King
Bass Book

Stuart Hamm -
The Early Years

Stuart Hamm -
Outbound & Beyond

Stu Hamm
The Book of Lies

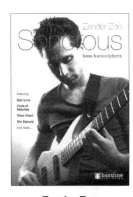

Zander Zon
Sonorous

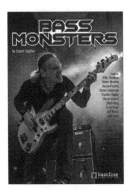

Bass Monsters

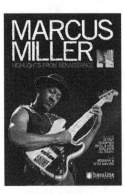

Marcus Miller
Highlights from
Renaissance

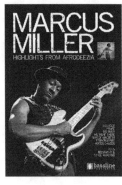

Marcus Miller
Highlights from
Afrodeezia

The Plectrum Bass
Book

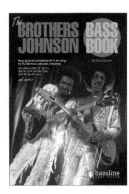

The Brothers Johnson
Bass Book

Available to order from **www.basslinepublishing.com** and from

ALSO AVAILABLE BASSLINE PUBLISHING VIDEO COURSES

After many years of writing a popular series of bass guitar tuition and transcription books, author and leading bass educator Stuart Clayton has created a series of instructional video courses. These are available via subscription to users all over the world.

Informed by Stuart's extensive experience as a teacher at one of the UK's top music schools, these courses are broken down into short, manageable lessons, with clear, attainable goals. Users can subscribe monthly or annually - subscriptions can be cancelled at any time.

MONTHLY* Subscription £7.99 per month
ANNUAL* Subscription £89 per year

Video Courses include:

Giants of Bass
Each course contains a full play-through of the piece, followed by section-by-section lessons on how to play in the style of well-known bassists including Billy Sheehan, Bootsy Collins, Carol Kaye, Flea, Mark King and many more.

Learning the Modes
This series of courses takes each of the modes and breaks it down into detail. Each course covers approaches to playing the mode all over the fingerboard and a range of exercises that it to use, so that you can hear the unique sound that each one offers.

Slap Bass
Beginner, Intermediate & Advanced
These courses are based on the popular *Ultimate Slap Bass* book and cover everything you need about this technique!

Scales and Arpeggios
Learn using the 'content over patterns' theory, avoiding the use of patterns and box shapes, and instead focuses on the notes.

Plectrum Course
This is a crucial technique to master for any professional bassist and this course is the perfect place to start.

Song Tutorials
Popular songs are broken down, section by section. Includes: 'Tommy the Cat' (Primus), 'Forget Me Nots' (Patrice Rushen), 'The Machine Stops' (Level 42), 'Hump de Bump' (Red Hot Chili Peppers) and more.

Tapping
Tapping is a rather unconventional technique, but in the right hands, it can be a valuable musical tool. Learn finger dexterity exercises, muting, and the best way to set up your bass for this technique.

New courses added regularly!

www.basslinepublishing.com

*Prices correct at time of printing but may be subject to change.

Made in United States
Troutdale, OR
12/26/2023

16445161R00055